AF486425

Cover created by
Amy Sturz

ISBN: 9798330437153
Blue Columbine Press

From Big Lakes
To Big Mountains

Amy Sturz

*For Justin, who has been
my strongest anchor in
the fiercest of storms.*

<u>Introduction:</u>
When I first started this poetry collection in 2021, it was going to be centered on my love for Lake Superior and the beauty of the North Shore. I was living in Duluth, Minnesota with the view of the lake right out my window. After years of seasonal work in the environmental education field, I finally earned a permanent position in my favorite city, right on the most beautiful lake in the world. It felt like a dream come true.

By 2023, I was under stress from juggling multiple jobs and trying to pay bills. After making multiple mistakes at the job I had initially moved out there for, I was fired. No one had asked about why I was making mistakes or what steps could be taken to help me manage my stress or workload.

The next 10 months were devastating for me. My mental health, which was already suffering, crashed further. My partner and I packed up our lives; he found work in Colorado while I moved in with his mother and returned to taking on summer jobs. If you're in the conservation field you know how frustrating and exhausting it can be. I placed my podcast, Supernatural Park, on hold for over a year.

By March of 2024, nearly a year after the loss of my job and move from Duluth, I found a park ranger position at a state park in Colorado and was able to move out where my partner was working. I fell in love with the new landscape I was living in and with that came healing and acceptance.

This poetry collection highlights my journey of mental and emotional health from the lakes of Minnesota to the mountains of Colorado. I am delighted to share with you the changes I experienced and the newfound love and connection I made with the Rocky Mountains.

-Park Ranger Amy
Creator of the podcast Supernatural Park

<u>I Love The Way You Are</u>
I love how you rage.
When natural forces
become too much

it is acceptable for you
to scream and roar.

I love the way
you cause destruction.

When you are violent and pull others down,
no one blames you
and there are no consequences.

I love your power.

When someone is too close
 to you on your bad days,
it's their own fault for being near the danger.

I love your dignity.

When you settle down
and have grown calm,
people still love you.

I wish I could be
more like you.

Collective Love

Around the world
you are honored and loved.

We show you our love
in different ways.

Not all are physical
and easy to do,

like picking up trash
and cleaning your shoreline.

Some advocate for you.

Some teach others about you.

Some write about you.

Some sing praises
of your power
and beauty.

Some hold celebrations
in your honor.

And one day,
long after we are gone,

future generations
will show how they love you.

<u>A Peptalk For Water and People</u>

You are a vast expanse of power
in an ever-changing world.

Still here, despite the extinction
of many species.

You can be fatal,
if you choose to be.

When storms cross your path,
never back down

and

don't

hold

back.

Never forget that you will go through many phases,
but your essence
will remain the same.

The molecules that make up your existence
cannot be destroyed;
just transformed into a more

powerful,

different,

but still the same,

beautiful you.

When I Am Surrounded By You

The freezing water envelopes me
as I duck under the waves.

My senses are shocked,
my breath quickens.

My heart skips a beat.

I come up gasping,
not for air
but from the rush I feel
of being embraced by you.

<u>The Beauty of Winter</u>

Most people would call this place frigid
but in this frozen wasteland
I find warmth.

Where others find misery in the cold
I find elation.

The stars above the lake shine bright
in the crystalized,
frozen air.

The full moon illuminates the water's beauty.

Showing that even in the depths of winter,
when all is silent and dark,

there's still a glimmer of wonder.

<u>Lifesaver</u>

There are some days
when I feel I won't make it.

The darkness weighs on me
like a heavy cloud.

I feel like I'm being pulled under
unable to breathe.

Grasping for a life saver,
anything to get me out.

But when I come to you
and sit beside your gentle waves;

when I listen to the rhythm of your water
crashing upon the shore,

the sun comes out and
my worries fade.

I feel the light again.

<u>Reincarnation</u>

My memory is faint,
this lake feels so familiar.
Have I been claimed
by it before?

Lake Superior,
is this memory I have
from a past life,
when I was twenty-four?

A crew of twenty-nine,
close as brothers we seemed
with families
and friends of our own.

From Wisconsin we came,
near Whitefish Bay
we would remain.
We thought for sure we'd return home!

On that dark, chilly night
in November we sailed
on clear waters
certain nothing could happen to us.

We left for our job
which was like any other:
a shipload of cargo
and filled with our trust.

The sky was clear
when we left for the day
filled with the taconite
Detroit would have soon.
All 200 pounds

of the bell's bronze
had been polished,
shining in the sunny afternoon.

But when nighttime fell,
black clouds descended
with screaming gales
and rogue waves we couldn't outrun.

Changing our course,
to Canada's shore
was the only thing
that could be done.

When it started to snow
we went down below
since no one could see anyway.

And when the ship swayed
Captain McSorley unafraid
declared "We are holding our own!"

The radar was tracked;
With the Anderson watching over,
we became obscured by sea return.

With a bump and a lurch
our signal was lost
never again to be discerned.

I remember the cold
and sinking below;
a sense of peace
overcoming fear.

Before my eyes, I felt paralyzed
when the sight of a white light appeared.

Someone once said
"You don't give up your dead."
And in this life
I may share the same fate.

It's hard to refuse you
when you shimmer so blue,
your beauty intoxicates!

East to the horizon,
we sail on you now.
I feel the water
and wind on my face.

I feel déjà vu within my soul
when there's a lurch of the bow.
I cling tight to the rail
Near Six Fathom Shoal.

The memories rush in,
like the water back then.
Will my life end
the same way again?

<u>Not For Sale</u>

You are a priceless treasure
and yet…
some people try to sell you.

You support life
and give beauty to the world.
How dare they try
to make money off of that?

As if you were only meant for a select, elite few
when you have been around to enjoy
for thousands of years
and are older than the concept of capitalism.

You are the reason
we are allowed to be here.

How could anyone put a price on that?

<u>Tributaries</u>

There is an endless system
for you out there.

Holding you together.

Little trickles like positive thoughts,

small streams like kind words,

mighty rivers like assertive actions,

feed into your body.

So whenever you're going through a drought
and feel like your levels are low
just remember:

support is coming your way.

<u>Untamed</u>

What would you be like if you
were wild and untamed?

Without the noise of life
and judgement
polluting your peace.

Would you be as free as the seagull that soars?
Or as loud as the storms?

Would you be as calm as the dew drops on trees
on a sunlit summer morn?

Close your eyes and listen to me.

You can be wild, and untamed, and all together, free.

<u>Shipwreck</u>

A century within this sea
I can't escape this misery.

On display so far away,
preserved for those to see.

You wrecked me here within your depths
on a journey I did take;

one fateful night, with no moonlight
you pulled me to my grave.

A tidal wave swept over and
pulled me down below.

Far beyond the light of day
where darkness seems to grow.

And now I sit here in silence
with my dead crew and the fish

and those who brave your icy waves
to dive if that's their wish.

<u>Origins</u>

Your story starts like all stories do:
at the beginning.

The land around you grew angry and erupted.

Fire and violence pulled you apart,
plumes of lava and rock spread out
to take over
further tearing you asunder.

They formed great cracks and fissures
and for millions of years,
fountains of flame flew into the air.

When finally, there was a moment of silence.

Magma ceased to flow,
as if there was no more.

The earth grew still as if the land was tired.

Ice came to cool your scars,
healing what had been broken.

Water flowed in
to fill the chasms
that were left behind.

And you were born.

<u>Sail Away</u>

I wish I could sail away from my troubles.

To simply float away,
peacefully.

Silently.

Away, from the worries of the world.

To let your gentle waters
and pleasant breeze
take me wherever you decide.

So that I may land in a place
without fear,
anxiety,
or worries.

But then…

that wouldn't be life, would it?

<u>Lake Superior Symphony</u>

A symphony of music plays
as the waves
crash the shore.

A crescendo begins
as the wind
whistles a tune.

The melody hits my ears
as dark clouds roll over.

The rhythm of thunder
drums in the distance.

The rain starts,
an adagio tempo
gently tapping
your surface,
in a slow moving beat.

It speeds up
until it hits the allegro,
fiercely hammering your wild waves.

And when I think
it can't fall any harder,
any stronger,

it turns into an rapid prestissimo;
drenching me and smacking my face

causing a tidal surge to crash into the shore,
forcing me to move away.

16

Lightning strikes the sky with fuoco,
fervently reminding me
that you aren't always gentle.

I watch from my balcony
as nature turns this display of weather
from a concert of elements
into a performance of your power.

Dark Beauty

I love watching you at night.

You seem to have your own glow

even without the light of the moon

bleaching out the inky darkness.

<u>Alone And At Peace</u>

I sit here
feeling small next to you.

It's just you and me together,
sitting with each other.

My senses are alert.
I take in your scent of clean, fresh, water.

The cold spray
crashing on the rocks
sprinkles my face.

It is peaceful here,
alone with you.

I would never want to be anywhere else.

<u>The Gull</u>

I am a gull
soaring above the water.

The wind beneath my wings
ruffles my feathers.

I don't feel the cold,
since my down keeps me warm.

If the water should spray me,
I will stay dry
thanks to the meticulous care
I take of my plumage.

And if I see a small fish? Lunch.

<u>More Like Me</u>

"Be more like me," she whispers softly
as her waves gently lap at the shoreline.

More soft, more fluid, more flexible.

"Be more like me!" she commands louder
retreating to come back
and crash into the land.

More forceful, more persistent,
only backing down
to come back stronger.

"BE MORE LIKE ME!"
she demands, screaming at me.

Her water pummels the rock,
eroding its surface;
taking her time but never stopping.

More powerful, more brutal, more pressing.

"Be more like me..."she sighs and quiets down.

More patient,
more accepting,
more forgiving of herself.

As she calms down for now, only to try again later.

<u>Split Rock Lighthouse</u>

I am a lighthouse
standing alone
and formidable
on this rocky cliff side.

Providing hope
and guidance
to those who are lost
in the dark.

My purpose
is to bring sailors safely
back to their families,
while also sparking the light of inspiration
in artists, poets, and musicians.

During the day,
millions come by to enjoy my beauty
and the coast I was made to watch.

At night it is just me, my light,
and the souls I guide in the dark.

Lake Superior Agate

Bands of marriage
between groundwater and rock
make up your form.

A sign of commitment
lasting thousands of years.

When You Were Young

When you were young
and nature had not yet been rearranged
by the hands of man,
your name was not known around the world.

It was only whispered sacredly
among the few who appreciated you.

When you were young,
the only lights that decorated your shores
were those of the sun, moon, and stars.

When you were young,
you were wild, fierce, and strong.
Capable of getting your way.

At least that part has not changed.

<u>Learn From The Animals</u>

The night before
a snowstorm is about to hit

nature grows silent.

The animals that know
who aren't already resting for winter
find a place to shelter.

Tucked in to the earth, safe from the weather.

Take advice from the animals, humans.
Heed the dark sky's warning
and stay home to wait it out.

<u>Back From Vacation</u>

Over the world I have traveled
through countries green and brown.

Through sand, and stone, and grassy knoll,
I am now homeward bound.

Near cliffs of copper rich,
to your shores of bluest hue.

Along the trails of fir and pine,
my path will always lead to you.

<u>Impossible</u>

A terrifying force such as yourself
demands respect
from those who live near you.

The fierce tidal wave
of icy water you constantly whip up,
slams over the rocks
and gushes as it returns.

Pulling whatever you snatch,
into your frozen depths.

Any logical person would stay away.

But for some,
such as me,
to keep my distance from you
is impossible.

<u>From The Perspective Of A Phoenix</u>

I died today.

It was my first time dying.

I had been told it would happen,
one day.

But no one had warned me
how painful it would be
or how suddenly it would occur.

I was resting in my nest,
watching the ships sail along
the wide, blue expanse of the sea
and preening my feathers.

Living out my routine like I did every day.

Suddenly,
in a painful and brilliant conflagration,
my body burned.

My nest caught fire.

Agony set me ablaze
bright enough to blind me.

My home,
my feathers,
everything I knew was burning
into an unrecognizable pile of ash.

There were no options,
no escape.

I had no choice but to surrender.

I think, maybe somewhere deep down,
I knew the end was near.

What had been so easy for so long
just grew uncomfortable.

I was tired more often
and could no longer find joy
in each day that I lived.

As I peek my small, featherless head
out of the pile of wreckage,
I blink.

Everything feels new and uncomfortable.
I need to relearn how to live.

I remember what it was like to fly,
to hunt, and forage;
but now I must put those things into practice again.

I crawl out of the ash pile
and look back at the remains
of what was once my home.

I can't stay here, I realize.
A new life requires a new nest.
I don't know where I will go next.

Maybe I will fly towards the sun,
where I was always meant to be.

<u>I Left My Heart In Lake Superior</u>

I took a boat out to the middle of the lake
and just sat there,
taking in the sight of endless water.

The clean, crisp air filled my lungs.

I closed my eyes and basked in the sun,
keeping the memory of warm, lakeside days
in my heart
putting all I've ever known
and loved
into it.

Then I carved it out with a knife made of seaglass.

I placed it in a mason jar,
weighed down with agates and
memories.

I breathed my soul into it,
filling it with dreams and wishes for the future.

I bottled it tightly and threw it in to the water.

Down it sank into the clear depths,
until it was out of sight,
at least 1300 feet below,
where only the shipwrecks and bottom dwellers
would be able to retrieve it.

Maybe someday I will be back; and yet perhaps not.

There is excitement and fear in the two tiny words "what if."

<u>Seaglass</u>

At first, you were carelessly discarded
thought to be a piece of trash.

You found your way into the lake,
its freezing waters enveloping you.

For years you stayed there
persistently battered
and pushed around by the waves.

Your trials smoothed your jagged edges,
the weathering of your form changed you.

And now as you sit upon this shoreline,
glinting in the sunlight,
you are seen as beautiful
and are considered treasure.

Although you didn't know it, you always were.

<u>Uncharted</u>

The path of life is uncharted.

I never really know where I am going.

I don't get to stay long.
I always keep moving
from one place to another.

But even if my journey takes me far from you,
you'll never be far from my heart.

<u>A New Lesson From Nature</u>

I came from the north,
the land of ice and snow;
the only wild and untamed place
that had no rules.

Or so I thought.

The inland seas, strong and wild, was true beauty.

Or so I thought.

But then I came out west,
and found a new kind of love
where the rocks keep their centuries old secrets.

The mountains show me
their own version strength
with intense snow storms
that melt by afternoon.

They show me
their own kind of lawless,
uncontrollable nature

with their freezing temperatures in the morning
turning into overwhelming dry heat
as the sun makes its way across the sky.

Also wild.

Also beautiful.

Towering Ponderosa

I look up at you and feel so insignificant.
What sights have you seen?

What stories do you have to share?

Oh great towering ponderosa!

What am I to you?

As you overlook nature from your vantage point,
I must appear small in size and power.

You will outlive me because you will last for 600 years,
while my lifespan is a mere 80,

a blink of an eye compared to you.

<u>Happy Accident</u>

I moved from Lake Superior to the Rocky Mountains.

Not out of choice, mind you.
Merely out of survival.

For being let go.

Despite the sorrow
and pain,

I have found pleasure
in the ruggedness of the Earth,
the fresh coolness
of the mountain streams,

And the sight of snowcapped peaks
that hold so much life
when you think everything is over.

<u>Tradeoff</u>

I traded the unpredictable lake
for unpredictable afternoon rain.

I traded the smell of sweet citrus
that wafts off of a Norwegian pine
for the sweet caramel scent of a ponderosa.

I traded the haunting call of a loon
searching for its mate
for the soft and mysterious hoot
of a spotted owl calling out to me.

I don't think I'd trade anything else
for these new treasures

<u>Trust Me</u>

Believe me when I say
"I do not love you any less."

I do miss you and the relaxing sound of your waves
rocking me to sleep.

I miss the jolts of joy I get
when I find sea glass
on your beaches.

But I have found a different kind of love
for the quiet strength
of the mountains.

You taught me how to flow and go with change.

Now I must learn to be strong
and steadfast in the face of it.

<u>I Can Still See The Northern Lights From Here</u>

The magic of the aurora,
 they say,
comes from the fire fox
running quickly through the snow.

It streaks with the glow of rubies and emeralds
as its tail whips ice crystals into the air
and sets them on fire.

Hunters dream of this beast,
searching for it
endlessly
to gain riches
that last a lifetime.

How rich am I then,
and how far it must have travelled,
for it to follow me here away from home.

Amid these red rocks.

<u>The Sand Lily</u>

Blurred red rocks of the hogbacks rise,
I wipe the teardrops from my eyes.

Coming out with broken heart I found
that hope did spring upon the ground.

For in between my feet did grow
a pale sand lily, white as snow.

And then a thought came to my head:
this plant in sand; it is not dead.

And in this harsh place I found myself in,
this dark despair that just might win,
if this flower so small and frail,
can grow in **sand**,

then I'll prevail.

<u>The Babblings of a Waterfall on Well Gulch Trail</u>

Crashing, gurgling waterfall,
splashing, running down rock wall.

Bubbling churning over stone,
carrying leaves away from home.

<u>Leave No Trace</u>

STOP!!!

What are you doing?

That flower that you are about to pick
is still in the young stages of life.

Sure, it's blooming
but it hasn't gone to seed.

It hasn't experienced
all that nature has to offer.

Would you want to be plucked early?
To miss out on a full life?

Allow yourself and the flower to grow,
to become what you and it were meant to be.

Please don't pick the wildwood flower.

<u>The Five Elements</u>

Maybe it's the rock hard earth
towering over this land,
that helps me feel confident enough
to draw boundaries.

Maybe it's the fluid water of the mountain streams
pushing its way through barriers
that helps me change course
when an obstacle stands in my path.

Maybe it's the crisp, pine scented air
Filling my lungs
that helps me take quiet moments for myself,
when I feel overwhelmed.

Maybe it's the needed wildfire
Burning the forests and grasslands
that runs in my veins
to help spark my creative determination to see this through.

Maybe it's the spirit of life I found,
within me and around,
that helped to chart my course and bring me here,
becoming more than I ever imagined.

<u>Reflection</u>

Water reflects the color of the objects above it.

What I currently see before me is this large,
rust colored behemoth.

It towers over the quiet, flat surface
casting its red glow over the clear lake.

It overwhelms the cloudless sky,
trumping the cerulean blue that we primarily see
enhancing the intensity of the color of the cliffs.

There is a scientific explanation for this.

But for now I'll just accept that nature is magic
and hope that I'm a reflection of it as well.

A Brand New Trail

It's different out here!

There is no sea glass to find,
no big expanse of wide blue lake to meet the horizon.

Instead, towering and impressive rocks
reach up to touch the sky.

The trails glitter and sparkle as if they were made of gold,
from the tiny mica crystal that litter the ground,
replacing the agates I'm so used to.

It's a good different.

An otherworldly different.

A new trail to discover.

A completely new path to take.

<u>It's Never The End</u>

Storms never last
but when they happen,
aren't they brilliant?

Streaks of lightning blaze
across the sky
determined to illuminate
the darkness
and to defy the shadows, sparking hope.

The wind howls to remind us
that we are not the only powerful force in the world
that we believe ourselves to be.
But we are more powerful than our mind tells us.

The lightning electrifies us,
driving us to continue onward through the pain
to show us that we can overcome what we go through,
even when it doesn't feel like it.

If it doesn't feel like it,
and sometimes it will,
let the storm remind you:

It's never the end

<u>My Favorite Place</u>

"When you're in your favorite place, how do you feel?"

Isle Royale National Park asked me, through their status on Facebook.

I thought hard. What was my favorite place anymore?

It used to be Lake Superior

Anywhere along Minnesota's North Shore.

But I think over time, things change.

It's a difficult question to answer for me.

Have I found my favorite place?

Is it the mountains now?

Perhaps it's wherever nature can bring out the best in me
and teach me that, wherever my favorite place is,

it's always beside me.

<u>Confessions of a Millennial Starseed</u>

I have a secret to confess:

I am not human.

I've come from the stars,
with iron in my blood.

I've come from the ocean
with salt water in my body.

I've come from nature,
buried in the dark as seed,
taking my own time to grow.

I've come from the ashes of wildfire,
that had burned the forest down
where that seed grew
but was able to return and thrive.

No, I am not human.

And after hearing this,
do you think you are?

<u>Acceptance</u>

I don't get to go there anymore.

I don't get to see the towering waves on a stormy day,
the kind that break over the barriers along the lake walk
and match the lake's rage with my own.

I don't get to find the peace I sought by the water,
when sadness overwhelmed me.

No, I don't get to go to Lake Superior anymore.

Instead I get to go somewhere else.

I get to call the mountains home now
and watch as the sun lights the canyons
with golden hues.

I get to go to the rolling foothills
with endless seas of waving grass,

the ponderosa pine forests
with scents of evergreen and vanilla.

And I get to shout out loud to the heavens
so that even those in
Duluth can hear me:

"I don't get to my old home anymore.
I am better off for it,
and now I can let go of my pain.

<u>Tectonically Speaking</u>

You are the same, exact result
of a process that has taken millions of years
to form the properties and structures
of earth's crust.

You have been stretched, thinned, crushed.
Folded into rigid plates.
Learning.
Transforming.

Surviving, thanks to the strong core inside you.

<u>A New Chapter</u>

The mountains whisper to me,
humming their seismic energy into my ear.

"You've made the right choice."

"You came to us by the will of the universe."

"We have so much to show you."

Not just what I can see
within their secretive,
craggy spaces.

But what I can see within myself.

The dark and harsh weathering it took
to create my final outcome.

"It's only going to get better from here."

Notes:
The original poem of "Reincarnation" was published on February 17, 2023 in Issue 1 of The Paper Crow online literary journal.

Acknowledgements:

Thank you to Lake Superior, who started this journey with me and the Rocky Mountains who helped to finish it.

Thank you to Justin for always sticking by me, even when I started to cry spontaneously, months after losing my job.

Thank you to freelance editor, Lorrie Wolf, who met with me to provide gentle encouragement, sound advice, and inspiration.

Thank you to the Gulo-Gulo Poetry Collective in Fort Collins, who offered me community and motivated me to continue writing.

Thank you to Great Lakes Aquarium for firing me. This collection would not have turned out the way it did otherwise.

<u>About the author</u>
Amy Sturz works as a park ranger somewhere in Colorado's Front Range. As a Certified Interpretive Guide through the National Association of Interpretation, she uses her skills as a park ranger to help people find a meaningful connection with nature through her poetry and her podcast, Supernatural Park.

She spends her time writing, teaching environmental education, and often searching for Bigfoot in the Rocky Mountains, who has yet to be found.

You can find her podcast on most streaming platforms, including Buzzsprout.

Park Ranger Amy accepts creative writing submissions from her listeners. If you would like to pay for an episode's monthly admission by submitting your work about nature or magic, please email your request to thesupernaturalpark@gmail.com

Follow her on social media at Facebook, Instagram, and X.

Facebook: https://www.facebook.com/SupernaturalPark/

Instagram: https://www.instagram.com/supernaturalpark/

X: @SNParkPodcast

Buzzsprout: https://feeds.buzzsprout.com/2024348.rss